Seventeen Songs For Children

Theresa M. Sull

PUBLICATION

Summary: SEVENTEEN SONGS FOR CHILDREN contains lyrics by Theresa Sull. All applicable copyrights and other rights are reserved worldwide. The text is set in Times New Roman, printed in the United States. All illustrations are provided by Liquidlibrary.

© Copyright 2021 Theresa M. Sull, Ph.D.

ISBN: 978-1-952302-94-7 (sc)
ISBN: 978-1-952302-95-4 (e)

All rights reserved. No part of this publication may be reproduced, stored in a retrieval system, or transmitted, in any form or by any means, electronic, mechanical, photocopying, recording, or otherwise, without the written prior permission of the author.

DEDICATION

To my granddaughter Abigail and my grandson Hudson,

whose smiles inspired me to publish these songs.

ACKNOWLEDGEMENTS

Singing, dancing, and gratitude for music were the gifts from my parents, Theresa and Michael Sudak. I thank those who support my writing, including my husband Gene Sull, daughters Linnet and Julia, and publishers of my books.

SEVENTEEN SONGS FOR CHILDREN

Theresa M. Sull M. Ph.D.

CONTENTS

MY FAVORITE FOODS 12
COOKING WITH RECIPES 13
SENSATIONAL 15
PUTTING THINGS AWAY 18
CLEANING UP 19
WASH, WASH, WASH 20
WASHING OFF THE DIRT 22
NAP-TIME LULLABY 23
STEP RIGHT UP MARCH 25
ROUND-UP 26
TEN LITTLE ANIMALS 28
OPENING A BOOK 29
WELCOME TO W 31
PICKING VEGETABLES 32
SEEING COLORS AND COUNTING 34
CREATURE COMFORTS 37
MY BUDDY, MY BODY 40

INTRODUCTION

Experts in human growth and education state that music can enhance children's development in at least six broad areas:

1) Gross Motor Skills that use large muscles for balance and movement.
2) Fine Motor Skills that use small muscles in eyes, fingers, and mouth, for seeing, touching, tasting, and talking
3) Cognitive Skills like concept formation, memory, and problem-solving
4) Language Skills like speaking, rhyming, and gaining vocabulary
5) Social Skills for co-operation, interaction, sharing space, turn-taking
6) Emotional Skills for feeling anger, anxiety, confusion, desire, disgust, empathy, envy, interest, joy, romance, surprise, triumph and more

Most people enjoy some types of music, but few folks realize that music helps children to develop, even before birth. As pregnant women dance and sing, rhythmic movements are felt by fetuses. This supports their brain development. Later in the pregnancy, a mother's voice becomes familiar.

Traditional tunes can connect children to humanity's past, and to cultures around the world. Modern music can connect children to their age-mates in other countries. Music has power to promote emotions in the agile and the clumsy, in short and tall people, in the young and the old.

How does music affect you personally? Are you a musician, a singer, a dancer, or a composer? Do you prefer Blues, Folk, Jazz, Pop, or Rock?

People can share music that originated in any populated continent. Children might have ancestors in Africa, Asia, Australia, Europe, North America, or South America.

MY FAVORITE FOODS

Oh, give me some fruit,
I don't give a hoot,
But my very favorite fruit,
Is banana!

An orange is OK,
Or an apple a day,
But my absolutely favorite
Is banana!

Make a vegetable plate,
Corn and green beans are great,
But my very favorite veggie
Is a carrot!

Purple eggplant is neat,
Yellow squash, or red beet,
But my crispy-crunchy favorite
Is a carrot!

COOKING WITH RECIPES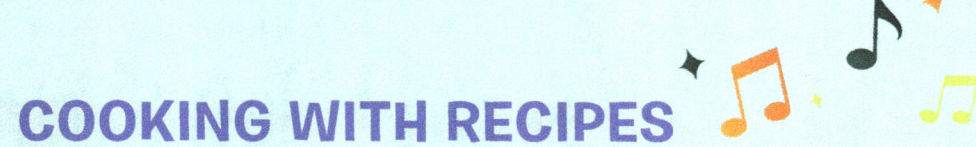

I took a quick look,
Inside of a book,
I found a good recipe,
Now we can cook!

So please wash your hands,
And gather our tools,
Because recipes work,
When we follow the rules!

SENSATIONAL

How do I look?
With my eyes on my face,
For watching and for seeing,
When you lead a chase.

How do I feel?
With my sensitive skin,
For rubbing and for hugging,
If you let me in.

How do I hear?
With my ears on my head,
For listening and for scratching,
When I lie in bed.

How do I smell?
With my nose in the front,
For following and tracking,
When I'm on the hunt.

How do I taste?
With my tongue in my mouth,

I'll gobble up your goodies,
If you don't watch out!

Honey is sweet,
And makes me smile,
But lemons, so sour,
Make me pucker for awhile. KISS! KISS!

PUTTING THINGS AWAY

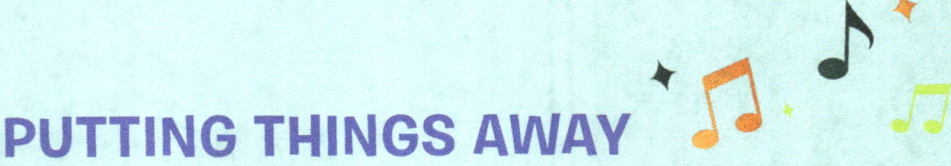

We're putting our blocks* away,
We hope it won't take all day,
We've got to get done,
To have even more fun!
We're putting our blocks away.

(*or books, cars, clay, clothes, dolls, toys, work)

CLEANING UP

I like the way that Abby is cleaning,
I like the way that Ethan is cleaning,
I like the way that Tanya is cleaning,
We're almost ready to have our lunch*!

(*or art, book, games, rest, snack, songs, walk)

WASH, WASH, WASH

Wash, wash, wash your hands (or ears, face, neck),
Many times a day,
Down the drain with soap and splashes,
Germs will go away!

WASHING OFF THE DIRT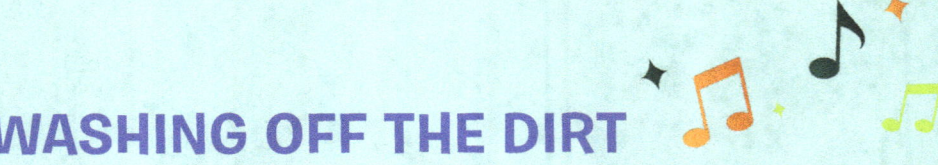

A rub-a-dub-dub,
An Abby in the tub,
We'll wash the dirt away. (*chorus*)

A rub-a-dub-dub,
A Huddy in the tub,
We'll wash the dirt away.

How did you get so dirty?
I'd really hate to say.
We'll fix it in a hurry,
We'll scrub that dirt away! (*repeat chorus*)

NAP-TIME LULLABY

Take a little nap, Tony, Tony,
Take a little nap and close your tired eyes.

Take a little nap, Abby, Abby,
When you wake up, there might be a surprise.*

(*such as painting, drawing, a book, a song, a visitor, a walk)

STEP RIGHT UP MARCH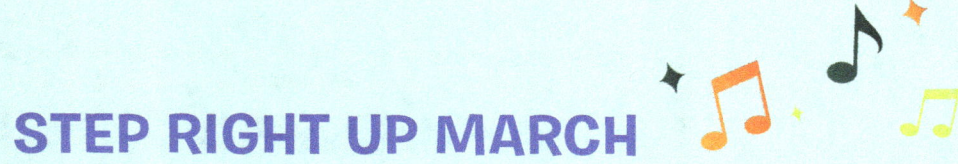

It's reading time, (Step right up, Sit right down.)
It's listening time, (Step right up, Sit right down.)
It's talking time, (Step right up, Sit right down.)
It's reading time right now!

ROUND-UP

Reading*, reading, reading,
Let's all do some reading,
Reading, reading, reading, right now.

Welcome to our reading,
We need you for our reading,
Reading, reading, reading, YEE-HA!

(*or Circle, Dancing, Listening, Meeting, Talking, Singing)

TEN LITTLE ANIMALS

One little, two little, three little animals,
Four little, five little, six little animals,
Seven little, eight little, nine little animals,
Ten little animal friends!

Ten little, nine little, eight little animals,
Seven little, six little, five little animals,
Four little, three little, two little animals,
One little animal friend!

OPENING A BOOK

When you open a book,
Certain things might fly out–
Things that can beckon,
Or things that can shout!

When you open a book,
You can even be caught,
By a thing that you might not
Have known that you sought!

WELCOME TO W

Welcome to W, Welcome.
Wonder what we will do, Welcome.
We wish for wizards and witches who will
Wave at our windows to give us a thrill.
Welcome to U and U, Welcome,
To W week, to W week, to W week!

PICKING VEGETABLES

Vegetables! Vegetables!
Will you pick (*have*) some of mine?
I've got zucchini* and I've got corn.
My vegetables are fine!

Vegetables! Vegetables!
Will you pick some of mine?
I've got some lettuce and I've got peas.
My vegetables are fine!

Vegetables! Vegetables!
Will you pick some of mine?
I've got potatoes and I've got kale.
My vegetables are fine!

Vegetables! Vegetables!
Will you pick some of mine?
I've got tomatoes and I've got leeks.
My vegetables are fine!

(*or broccoli, cucumber, pumpkins, onions, squash)

SEEING COLORS AND COUNTING

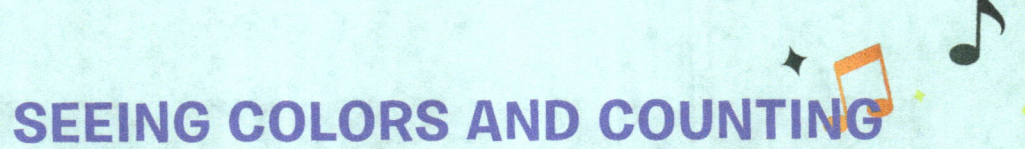

What if we couldn't see colors,
So a sunset was no longer red?
The blue sky no longer reflected blue seas,
And even a rainbow looked dead?

What if all colors were different?
If brown was the brightest we'd seen?
If a goldfinch was gray or a bluebird was black?
If the grass wasn't yellow or green?

What if all mountains were turquoise?
If lavender flowers were beige?
If purple was yellow and silver was white?
And the greens only chartreuse or sage?

What if we couldn't use numbers,
To count all the objects we find?
Fingers and toes couldn't measure amounts,
Which could really put kids in a bind!

What if most numbers were seven?
So to have only one car was rare?
We'd run out of metal and plastic,
But an automobile wouldn't care.

On this planet called earth we have sunshine,
To help us see creatures and plants,
And thank goodness we'll always have numbers,
To compare tall sequoias to ants!

CREATURE COMFORTS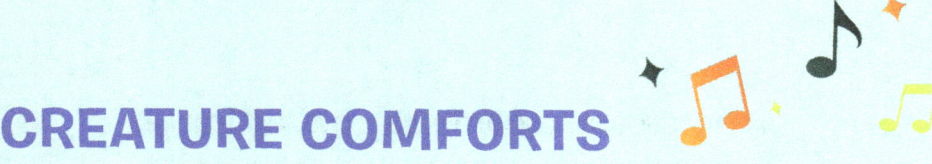

Flamingos and egrets and eagles and moths,
Are creatures that fly through the sky.
They soar and they hurl and they dive from the clouds,
Hunting their prey from on high.

(Our fellow creatures know just what they need.
"The earth is our home, so be careful," they plead.)*

Lobsters and starfish and swordfish and whales,
Are creatures that live in the sea.
Some skim over seaweed, some hide in the sand,
They're hiding from monsters like me.

Choral and crayfish and turtle and eel,
Are creatures who love to be wet.
A walrus, a crocodile, seahorse or seal,
Such animals don't make good pets!

Penguin and polar bear, walrus and seal,
Are creatures that slide on the ice,
With Inuit folk wearing parkas and boots,
Who think that cold weather is nice.

A horse and a camel, a cow, a giraffe,
Are creatures that walk on the land.
A zebra, an elephant, lizard or yak,
Prefers grazing grass over sand.

Bonobos, Chimpanzees, Lemurs, Orangutans,
All are primates that can swing in high trees.
Like Gibbons, Gorillas, Monkeys, and People,
Most are sociable, generally aiming to please.

(*Repeat this two-line chorus after each verse.)

MY BUDDY, MY BODY

I need my feet, to hold me up,
They also help me run and jump.
My feet are things I'd hate to lose,
Because I love my socks and shoes.

I need my knees, to bend and lock,
So when I move I walk tick-tock.
Without my knees I could not sit,
Or exercise to keep me fit.

I need my hips, to sway and stop,
My waist must bend or I'd just flop.
I use my waist and hips to dance,
They also help hold up my pants!

I need my head, to hold my face,
It also keeps my hair in place.
My head's my most important part,
My brain's inside, that's why I'm smart!

ABOUT THE AUTHOR

A career educator, Theresa M. Sull taught in both preschools and colleges, and consulted to parents and other teachers in child care centers, public schools, and university programs. Theresa sees herself as a bridge connecting early childhood theory and research with the classrooms and family homes where young children are learning through play.

Theresa Sull earned a doctorate in Educational Psychology from the University of North Carolina at Chapel Hill, not far from her home on the Eno River. She holds a master's degree in Teaching Young Children with Special Needs, from Wheelock College in Boston, and undergraduate degrees from the State University of New York at New Paltz, in English and Day Care Administration.

Dr. Sull published books about children's development, their communication, education, and literacy. She resides in historic Hillsborough, North Carolina, where she watches wildlife in her backyard. Theresa can be reached at tcandgenesull@gmail.com.

www.ingramcontent.com/pod-product-compliance
Lightning Source LLC
Chambersburg PA
CBHW081758100526
44592CB00015B/2482